West Chicago Public Library District
118 West Washington
West Chicago, IL 60185-2803
Phone # (630) 231-1552
Fax # (630) 231-1709

Bilingual Picture Dictionaries

My First Book of
Greek
Words

by Katy R. Kudela

Translator: Translations.com

apple
μήλο
(ME-lo)

CAPSTONE PRESS
a capstone imprint

Table of Contents

How to Use This Dictionary

This book is full of useful words in both Greek and English. The English word appears first, followed by the Greek word. Look below each Greek word for help to sound it out. Try reading the words aloud.

Topic Heading in English

Topic Heading in Greek

Word in English
Word in Greek
(pronunciation)

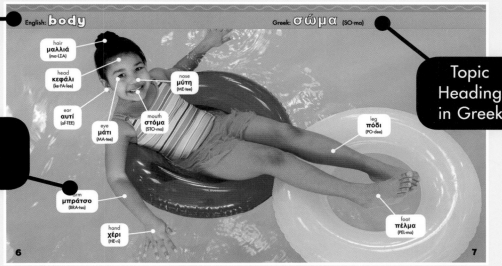

English: **body**

Greek: σώμα (SO-ma)

hair
μαλλιά
(ma-LIA)

head
κεφάλι
(ke-FA-lee)

nose
μύτη
(ME-tee)

ear
αυτί
(af-TEE)

eye
μάτι
(MA-tee)

mouth
στόμα
(STO-ma)

leg
πόδι
(PO-dee)

arm
μπράτσο
(BRA-tso)

hand
χέρι
(HE-ri)

foot
πέλμα
(PEL-ma)

6

7

Notes about the Greek Language

The Greek alphabet has 24 letters. It is the oldest alphabet still in use.

The Greek language uses accents shown with a '. The accent means that your voice should stress the vowel with the accent.

There are sounds that do not exist in Greek. These sounds include:
[sh] as in "shop"　　　　[z] as in "pleasure"　　　[ch] as in "church"

Most of the Greek letter proununciations have sounds that are like English. To read the Greek characters, look at the pronunciation.

English: **family**

uncle
θείος
(THE-os)

mother
μητέρα
(mee-TE-ra)

cousin
εξάδελφος
(e-KSA-del-fos)

aunt
θεία
(THE-a)

baby
μωρό
(mo-RO)

Greek: **ΟΙΚΟΓΈΝΕΙΑ** (e-ko-GE-ne-ea)

grandmother
γιαγιά
(gia-GIA)

father
πατέρας
(pa-TE-ras)

grandfather
παππούς
(pa-POUS)

brother
αδερφός
(a-der-FOS)

sister
αδερφή
(a-der-FEE)

5

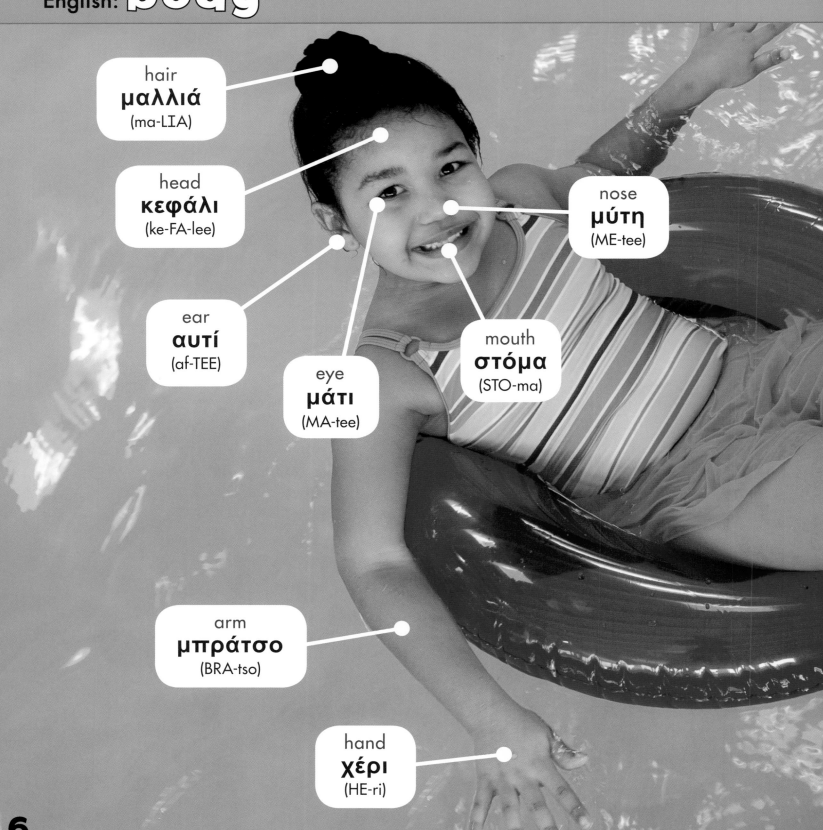

hair
μαλλιά
(ma-LIA)

head
κεφάλι
(ke-FA-lee)

ear
αυτί
(af-TEE)

eye
μάτι
(MA-tee)

nose
μύτη
(ME-tee)

mouth
στόμα
(STO-ma)

arm
μπράτσο
(BRA-tso)

hand
χέρι
(HE-ri)

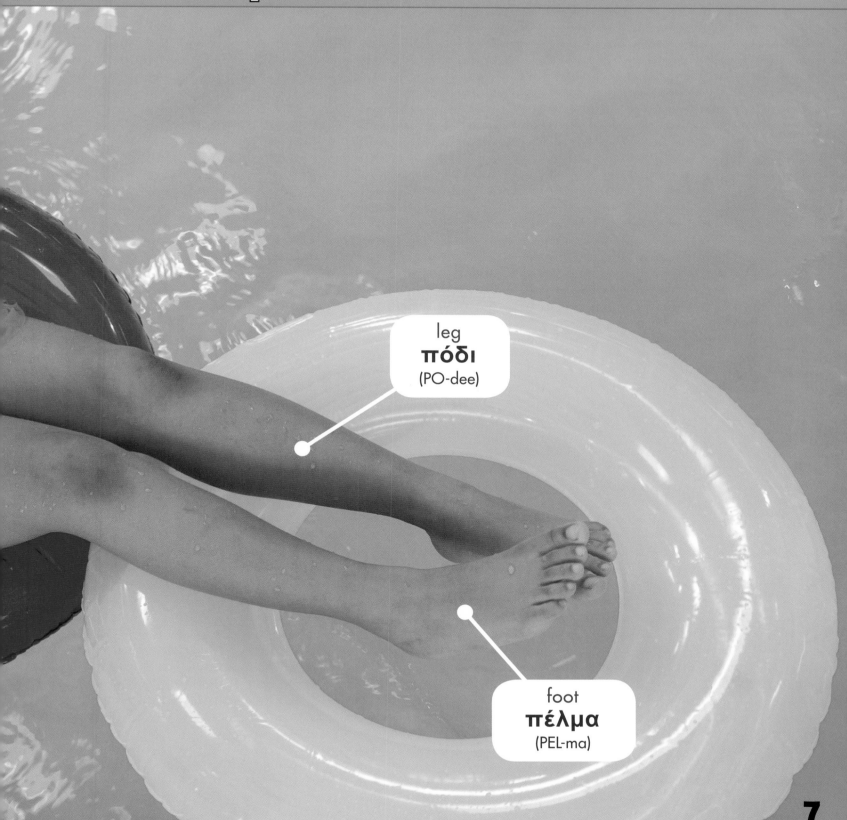

leg
πόδι
(PO-dee)

foot
πέλμα
(PEL-ma)

7

coat
παλτό
(pal-TO)

pajamas
πυτζάμα
(pi-JA-ma)

shorts
σορτσάκι
(sor-TSA-kee)

boot
μπότα
(BO-ta)

8

shoe
παπούτσι
(pa-POO-tsee)

hat
καπέλο
(ka-PE-lo)

pants
παντελόνι
(pan-te-LO-nee)

sock
κάλτσα
(KAL-tsa)

dress
φόρεμα
(FO-re-ma)

shirt
πουκάμισο
(poo-KA-mee-so)

9

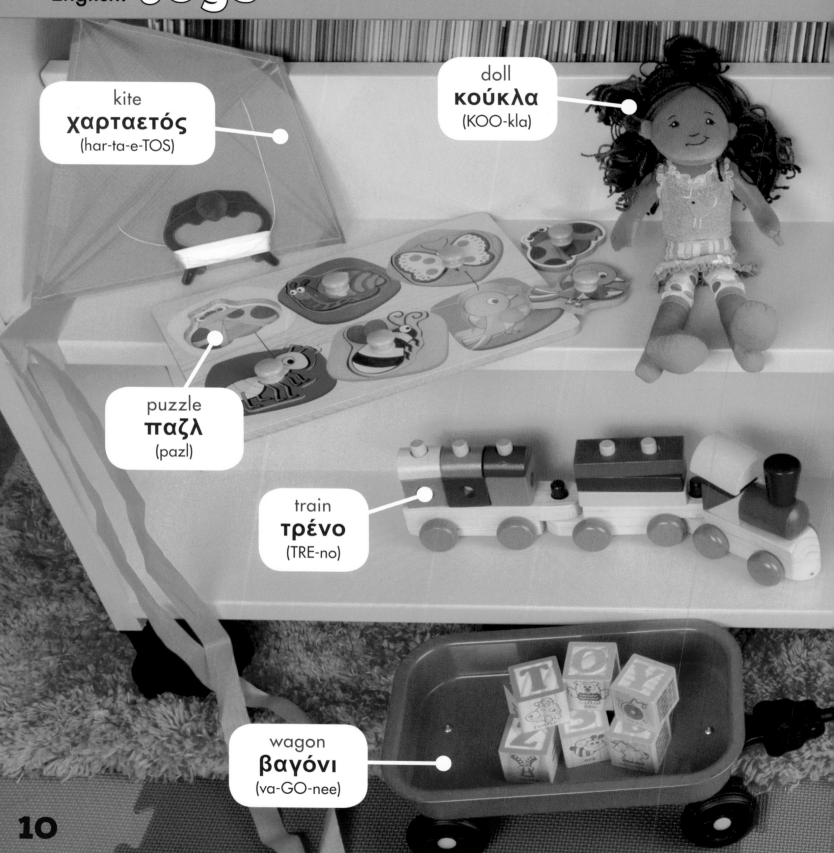

kite
χαρταετός
(har-ta-e-TOS)

doll
κούκλα
(KOO-kla)

puzzle
παζλ
(pazl)

train
τρένο
(TRE-no)

wagon
βαγόνι
(va-GO-nee)

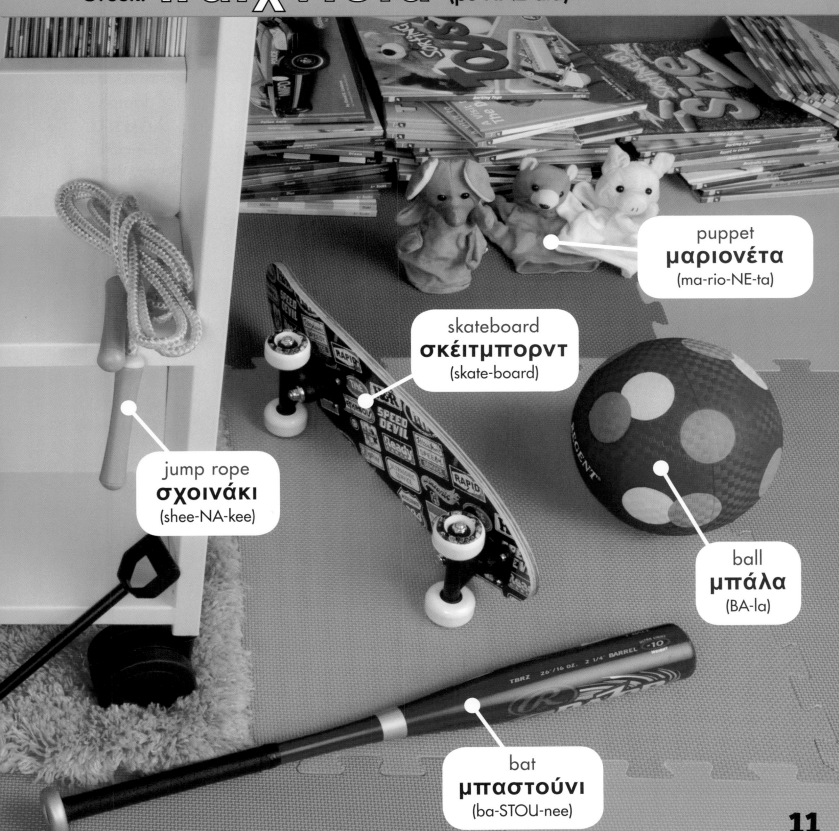

Greek: **παιχνίδια** (pe-HNI-dia)

puppet
μαριονέτα
(ma-rio-NE-ta)

skateboard
σκέιτμπορντ
(skate-board)

jump rope
σχοινάκι
(shee-NA-kee)

ball
μπάλα
(BA-la)

bat
μπαστούνι
(ba-STOU-nee)

11

window
παράθυρο
(pa-RA-thee-ro)

picture
φωτογραφία
(fo-to-gra-FI-a)

lamp
λάμπα
(LA-mpa)

dresser
ντουλάπι
(doo-LA-pee)

curtain
κουρτίνα
(koor-TI-na)

blanket
κουβέρτα
(ku-VER-ta)

Greek: κρεβατοκάμαρα (kre-va-to-KA-ma-ra)

door
πόρτα
(POR-ta)
pillow
μαξιλάρι
(ma-xi-LA-ri)
bed
κρεβάτι
(kre-VA-ti)
rug
χαλάκι
(ha-LA-kee)

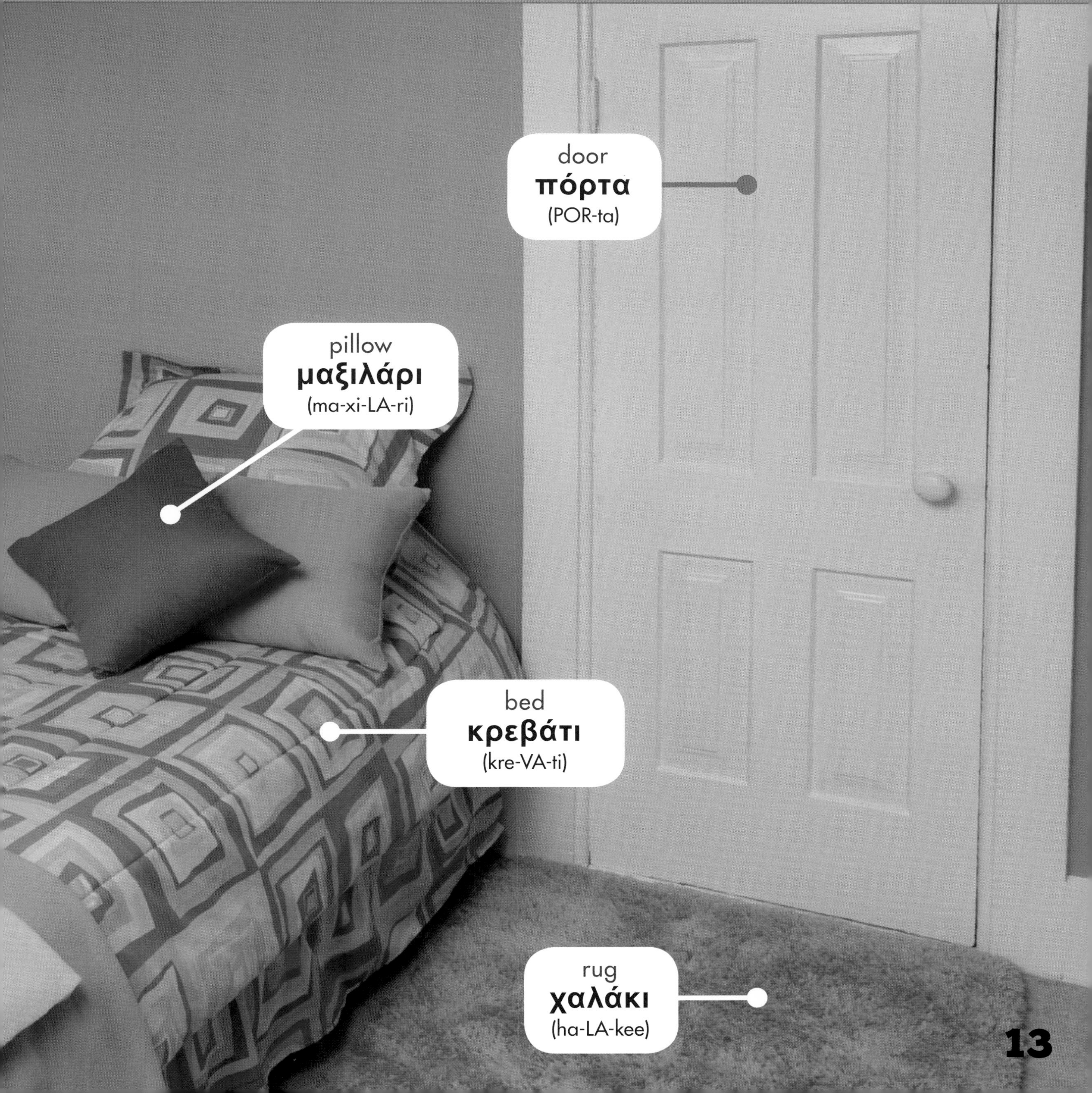

bathtub
μπανιέρα
(ba-NIE-ra)

soap
σαπούνι
(sa-POO-ni)

toilet
λεκάνη τουαλέτας
(le-KA-ni too-a-LE-tas)

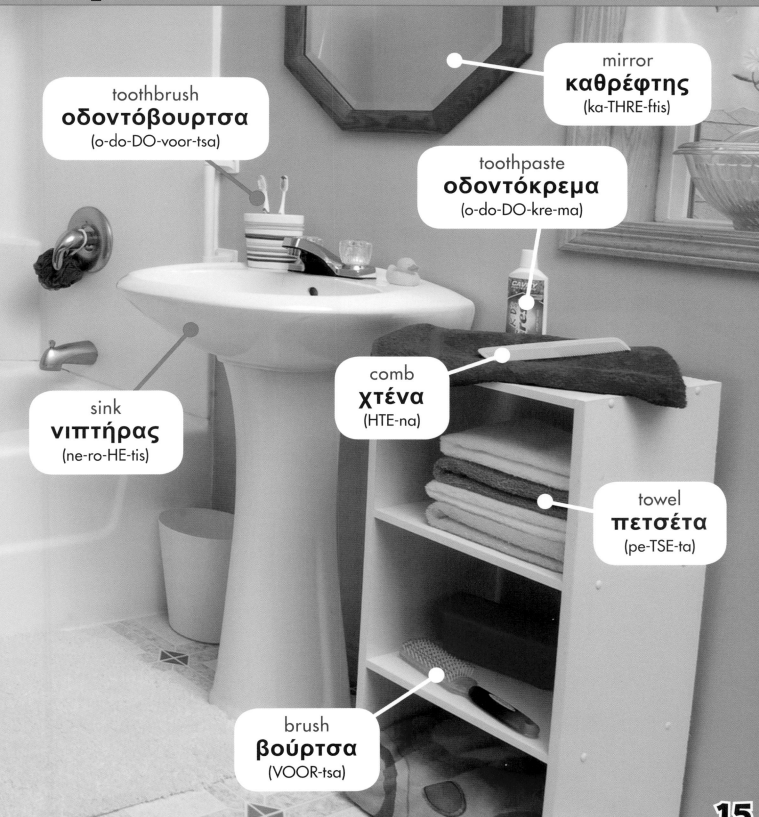

mirror
καθρέφτης
(ka-THRE-ftis)

toothbrush
οδοντόβουρτσα
(o-do-DO-voor-tsa)

toothpaste
οδοντόκρεμα
(o-do-DO-kre-ma)

comb
χτένα
(HTE-na)

sink
νιπτήρας
(ne-ro-HE-tis)

towel
πετσέτα
(pe-TSE-ta)

brush
βούρτσα
(VOOR-tsa)

15

pot
κατσαρόλα
(ka-tsa-RO-la)

stove
εστία
(e-STI-a)

bowl
μπολ
(bol)

oven
φούρνος
(FOOR-nos)

16

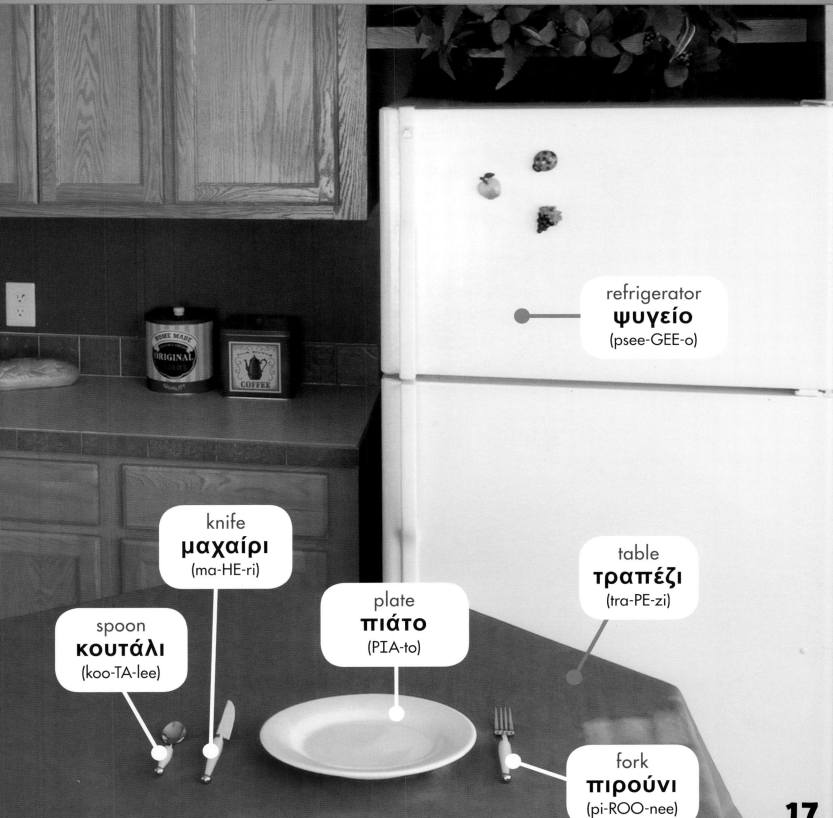

Greek: **κουζίνα** (koo-ZI-na)

refrigerator
ψυγείο
(psee-GEE-o)

knife
μαχαίρι
(ma-HE-ri)

table
τραπέζι
(tra-PE-zi)

spoon
κουτάλι
(koo-TA-lee)

plate
πιάτο
(PIA-to)

fork
πιρούνι
(pi-ROO-nee)

17

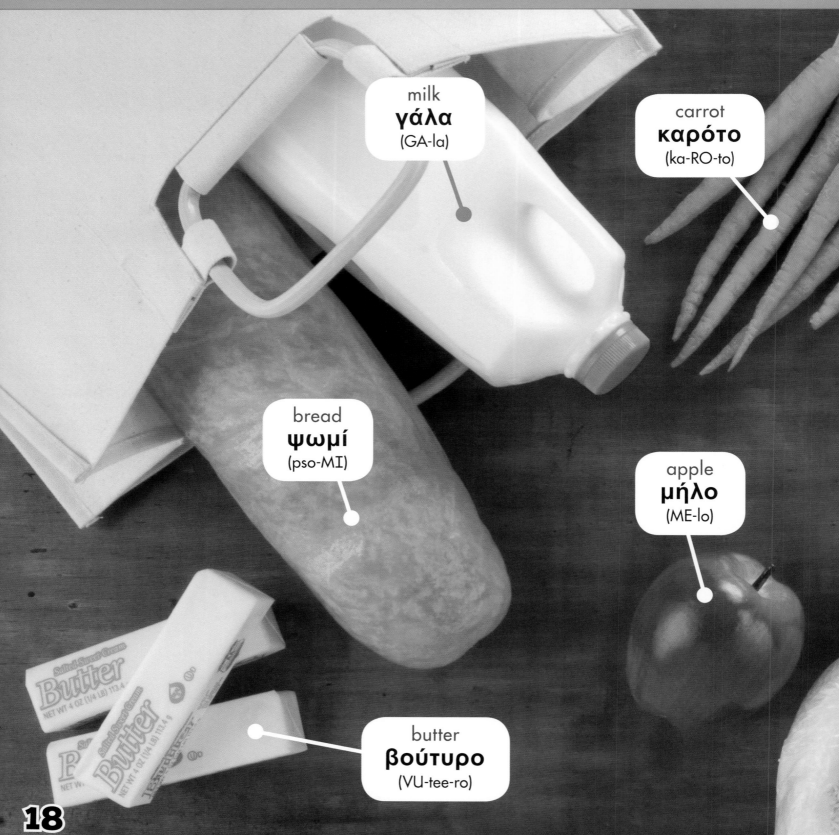

milk
γάλα
(GA-la)

carrot
καρότο
(ka-RO-to)

bread
ψωμί
(pso-MI)

apple
μήλο
(ME-lo)

butter
βούτυρο
(VU-tee-ro)

Greek: **φαγητό** (fa-gee-TO)

egg
αβγό
(av-GO)

pea
μπιζέλι
(bee-ZE-lee)

orange
πορτοκάλι
(por-to-KA-li)

sandwich
σάντουιτς
(SAN-toueets)

rice
ρύζι
(RE-zee)

19

tractor
τρακτέρ
(tra-KTER)

hay
σανός
(sa-NOS)

fence
φράχτης
(FRA-htees)

farmer
αγρότης
(a-GRO-tees)

sheep
πρόβατο
(PRO-va-to)

pig
γουρούνι
(gu-RU-nee)

20

horse
άλογο
(A-lo-go)

barn
αχυρώνας
(a-hee-RO-nas)

cow
αγελάδα
(a-ge-LA-da)

chicken
κοτόπουλο
(ko-TO-poo-lo)

21

leaf
φύλλο
(FE-lo)

butterfly
πεταλούδα
(pe-ta-LOO-da)

flower
λουλούδι
(lu-LU-dee)

shovel
φτυάρι
(FTIA-ree)

bird
πουλί
(pu-LE)

worm
σκουλήκι
(sku-LE-kee)

22

plant
φυτό
(fee-TO)

grass
γρασίδι
(gra-SE-dee)

dirt
βρωμιά
(vro-MIA)

seed
σπόρος
(SPO-ros)

Edamame Green Soybean
Tohya
Glycine max

$2.99
Net Weight
15 grams
80 days
Warm season
crop - plant after
last chance of
spring frost

So high in
protein, it is
called "the meat
without bones".
Boiled, beans
are popped out
of the pod into
your mouth for
a culinary
delight!

Chives

Botanie

23

purple
βιολετί
(vio-le-TI)

brown
καφέ
(ka-FE)

orange
πορτοκαλί
(por-to-ka-LI)

white
άσπρο
(A-spro)

red
κόκκινο
(KO-ki-no)

black
μαύρο
(MA-vro)

24

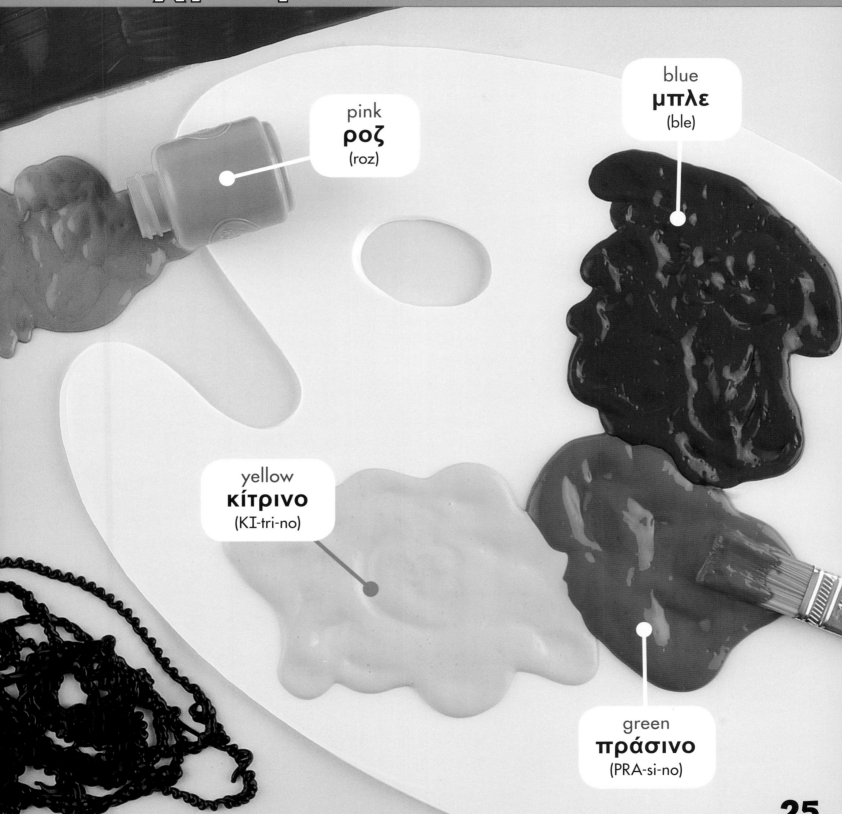

pink
ροζ
(roz)

blue
μπλε
(ble)

yellow
κίτρινο
(KI-tri-no)

green
πράσινο
(PRA-si-no)

teacher
δασκάλα
(da-SKA-la)

book
βιβλίο
(vi-VLI-o)

desk
γραφείο
(gra-FE-o)

pencil
μολύβι
(mo-LE-vi)

crayon
κραγιόνι
(kra-GIO-ni)

map
χάρτης
(HAR-tis)

clock
ρολόι
(ro-LO-ee)

computer
υπολογιστής
(ee-po-lo-gi-STIS)

chair
καρέκλα
(ka-RE-kla)

paper
χαρτί
(har-TE)

27

traffic light
φανάρι
(fa-NA-ree)

library
βιβλιοθήκη
(vee-vlee-o-THE-kee)

store
κατάστημα
(ka-TA-stee-ma)

LIBRARY

ONE WAY

Tuesday 2:00-5:00
Thursday 2:00-6:00

bicycle
ποδήλατο
(po-DE-la-to)

car
αυτοκίνητο
(a-fto-KE-nee-to)

28

Greek: **πόλη** (PO-lee)

tree
δέντρο
(DE-ntro)

bus
λεωφορείο
(le-o-fo-REE-o)

park
πάρκο
(PAR-ko)

street
δρόμος
(DRO-mos)

sign
πινακίδα
(pee-na-KE-da)

STOP

29

Numbers • Αριθμοί (a-rith-MOI)

1. one • **ένα** (E-na)

2. two • **δύο** (DI-o)

3. three • **τρία** (TRI-a)

4. four • **τέσσερα** (TE-se-ra)

5. five • **πέντε** (PE-nte)

6. six • **έξι** (E-ksi)

7. seven • **εφτά** (e-FTA)

8. eight • **οχτώ** (o-HTO)

9. nine • **εννιά** (e-NIA)

10. ten • **δέκα** (DE-ka)

Useful Phrases • Χρήσιμες φράσεις (HRI-si-mes FRA-sis)

yes • **ναι** (ne)

no • **όχι** (O-hi)

hello • **γεια** (GEIA-sou)

good-bye • **αντίο** (a-DI-o)

good morning • **καλημέρα** (ka-li-ME-ra)

good night • **καληνύχτα** (ka-li-NI-hta)

please • **παρακαλώ** (pa-ra-ka-LO)

thank you • **ευχαριστώ** (ef-ha-ri-STO)

excuse me • **με συγχωρείτε** (me seen-ho-REE-te)

My name is _____. • **Με λένε** _____. (me LE-ne)

Read More

Marsh, Carole. *It Really Is Greek to Me!: Greek for Kids.* Peachtree City, Ga.: Gallopade International, 2004.

Papaloizos, Theodore C. *My First Book.* Silver Spring, Md: Papaloizos Publications, 2007.

Internet Sites

FactHound offers a safe, fun way to find Internet sites related to this book. All of the sites on FactHound have been researched by our staff.

Here's all you do:

Visit www.facthound.com

Type in this code: 978142959666

 Check out projects, games and lots more at
www.capstonekids.com

A+ Books are published by Capstone Press,
151 Good Counsel Drive, P.O. Box 669, Mankato, Minnesota 56002.
www.capstonepub.com

Books published by Capstone Press are manufactured with paper
containing at least 10 percent post-consumer waste.

Library of Congress Cataloging-in-Publication Data
Kudela, Katy R.
    My first book of Greek words / by Katy R. Kudela.
    p. cm. — (A+ Books, Bilingual picture dictionaries)
    Includes bibliographical references.
    Summary: "Simple text paired with themed photos invite the reader to learn to speak Greek"—
Provided by publisher.
    ISBN 978-1-4296-5966-6 (library binding)
    ISBN 978-1-4296-6171-3 (paperback)
    1. Picture dictionaries, Greek (Modern) 2. Picture dictionaries, English. 3. Greek language,
Modern.—Dictionaries, Juvenile—English. 4. English language—Dictionaries, Juvenile—Greek language,
Modern. I. Title.
PA1139.E5K83 2011
489'.3321—dc22   2010029468

Credits
Lori Bye, book designer; Wanda Winch, media researcher; Eric Manske, production specialist

Photo Credits
Capstone Studio/Gary Sundermeyer, cover (pig), 20 (farmer with tractor, pig)
Capstone Studio/Karon Dubke, cover (ball, sock), 1, 3, 4–5, 6–7, 8–9, 10–11, 12–13, 14–15,
    16–17, 18–19, 22–23, 24–25, 26–27
Image Farm, back cover, 1, 2, 31, 32 (design elements)
iStockphoto/Andrew Gentry, 28 (main street)
Photodisc, cover (flower)
Shutterstock/Adrian Matthiassen, cover (butterfly); David Hughes, 20 (hay); Eric Isselee,
    20–21 (horse); hamurishi, 28 (bike); Ievgeniia Tikhonova, 21 (chickens); Jim Mills, 29
    (stop sign); Kelli Westfal, 28 (traffic light); Margo Harrison, 20 (sheep); MaxPhoto, 21
    (cow and calf); Melinda Fawver, 29 (bus); Robert Elias, 20–21 (barn, fence); Vladimir
    Mucibabic, 28–29 (city skyline)

Note to Parents, Teachers, and Librarians
Learning to speak a second language at a young age has been shown to improve overall
academic performance, boost problem-solving ability, and foster an appreciation for other
cultures. Early exposure to language skills provides a strong foundation for other subject
areas, including math and reasoning. Introducing children to a second language can help
to lay the groundwork for future academic success and cultural awareness.

Printed in the United States of America in North Mankato, Minnesota.
092010   005933CGS11

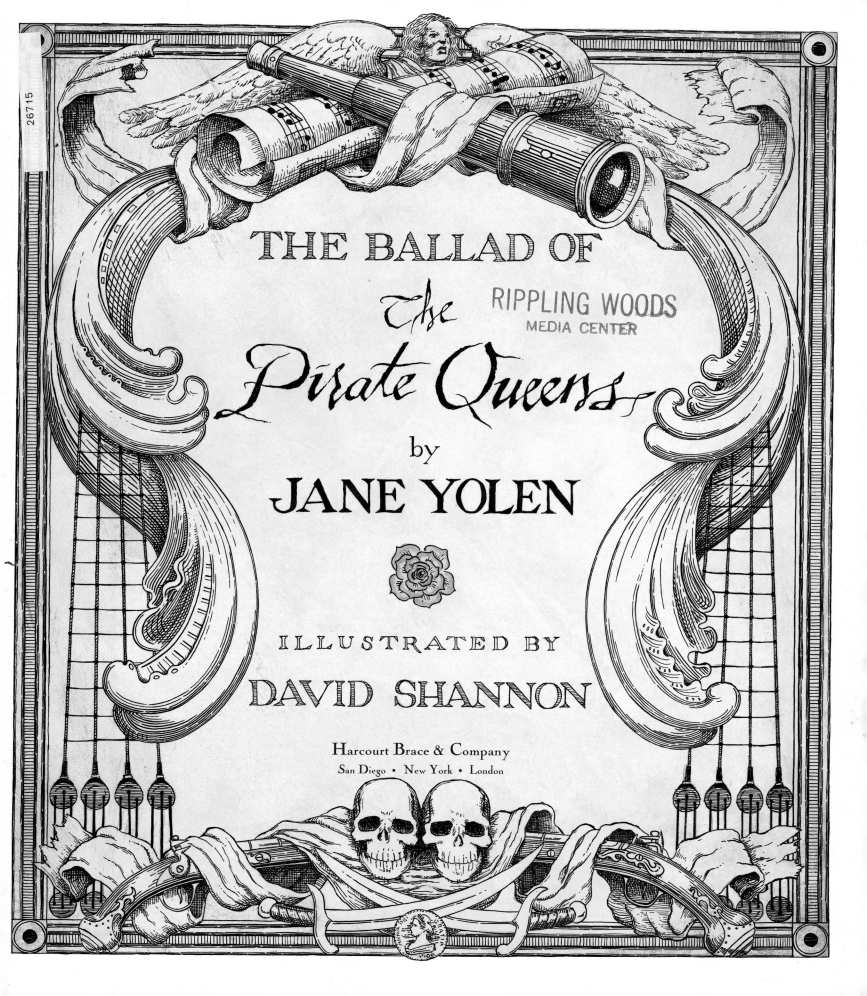

THE BALLAD OF

The

Pirate Queens

by

JANE YOLEN

ILLUSTRATED BY

DAVID SHANNON

Harcourt Brace & Company
San Diego • New York • London

For Bonnie, her book
— J. Y. and D. S.

Requests for permission to make copies of any part of the work
should be mailed to: Permissions Department, Harcourt Brace & Company,
6277 Sea Harbor Drive, Orlando, Florida 32887-6777.

Library of Congress Cataloging-in-Publication Data
Yolen, Jane.
The ballad of the pirate queens/written by Jane Yolen;
illustrated by David Shannon.—1st ed.
p. cm.
Summary: Two women who sailed with "Calico Jack" Rackham and his pirates in the
early 1700s do their best to defend their ship while the men on board are busy drinking.
ISBN 0-15-200710-5
1. Bonney, Anne, b. 1700—Juvenile fiction. 2. Reade, Mary, d.
1720?—Juvenile fiction. [1. Bonney, Anne, b. 1700—Fiction.
2. Reade, Mary, d. 1720?—Fiction. 3. Pirates—Fiction.]
I. Shannon, David, 1959– ill. II. Title.
PZ7.Y78Bal 1995
[Fic]—dc20   94-7874

C E G H F D

Printed in Singapore

The illustrations in this book were done in acrylic paint on illustration board.
The display type was hand-lettered by the illustrator.
The text type was set in Nicolas Cochin by Thompson Type, San Diego, California.
Color separations by Bright Arts, Ltd., Singapore
Printed and bound by Tien Wah Press, Singapore
Production supervision by
Warren Wallerstein and Ginger Boyer
Designed by Lisa Peters

Spelling was not regular in the days of Anne Bonney and Mary Reade.

In some reports Anne and Reade are spelled without *e*'s at the end.

Port Maria ~ 1720

THE AUTUMN SEAS are deep and dark
In Port Maria Bay;
The tunny fish all leap and sport
Around the bustling cay.

"What news, what news?" the people cry.
"What news bring you to town?"
"The governor has sent his ships
To pull the pirates down."

"The governor has sent his ships
With cannon all a-bristle,
And on the silver sea they sail
Just like a stinging thistle."

And silver the coins and silver the moon,
Silver the waves on the top of the sea,
When the pirate ship comes sailing in,
That gallant *Vanity*.

The Vanity

Now one small sloop that flew the black
Was Rackham's *Vanity*,
And it was manned by twelve brave lads
Upon the roiling sea.

When it was far and far from shore
Those twelve brave lads were ten,
For only on the sloop was known
That two of them weren't men.

Though only on the sloop was known
That one was bonny Anne,
And one was Mary Reade who dressed
Exactly like a man.

Anne Bonney

Mary Reade

"What news, what news?" the people cry.
"What news bring you to town?"
"Barnet has sailed his man-o'-war
To pull the pirates down."

"Barnet has sailed the *Albion*
Upon the autumn sea
To capture Rackham—'Calico Jack'—
And the gallant *Vanity*."

He slipped the western point of land,
All on that autumn day,
And there the pirates lay in wait
For their accustomed prey.

Barnet on board the Albion

The Albion

And silver the coins and silver the moon,
Silver the waves on the top of the sea,
When the pirate ship comes sailing in,
That gallant *Vanity*.

The autumn seas were deep and dark
Near Point Negril that day.
Two pirates stood upon the deck;
The rest, below, did play.

The rest, below, did drink and sport,
While up above the two
Kept silently their daily watch
For *Vanity* and crew.

"A ship, a ship!" did Mary cry.
And Anne cried, "Man-o'-war!"
But down below, Jack and his men
Did drink and sport some more.

The Albion engages the Vanity

And silver the coins and silver the moon,
Silver the waves on the top of the sea,
When the pirate ship comes sailing in,
That gallant *Vanity*.

"A ship, a ship!" did Mary cry.
"Come up and lend a hand."
    But Rackham and his merry men
    Came not to her command.

"A ship, a ship!" then Anne cried, too.
"Or else we will be taken."
    But Rackham and his merry men
    Their duties had forsaken.

So shoulder to shoulder and back to back,
Stood Mary and stood Anne;
    Never was it said that they
    Were feared of any man.

Defending the Varsity

Then one and two and through and through
Barnet's men plied their blades,
Until they'd overpowered both
Those doughty pirate maids.

Until Barnet had overcome
And brought them both to shore
Aboard the mighty *Albion*,
That bristly man-o'-war.

"What news, what news?" the people cry.
"What news bring you to town?"
"The *Vanity* is captured,
And two pirate queens brought down."

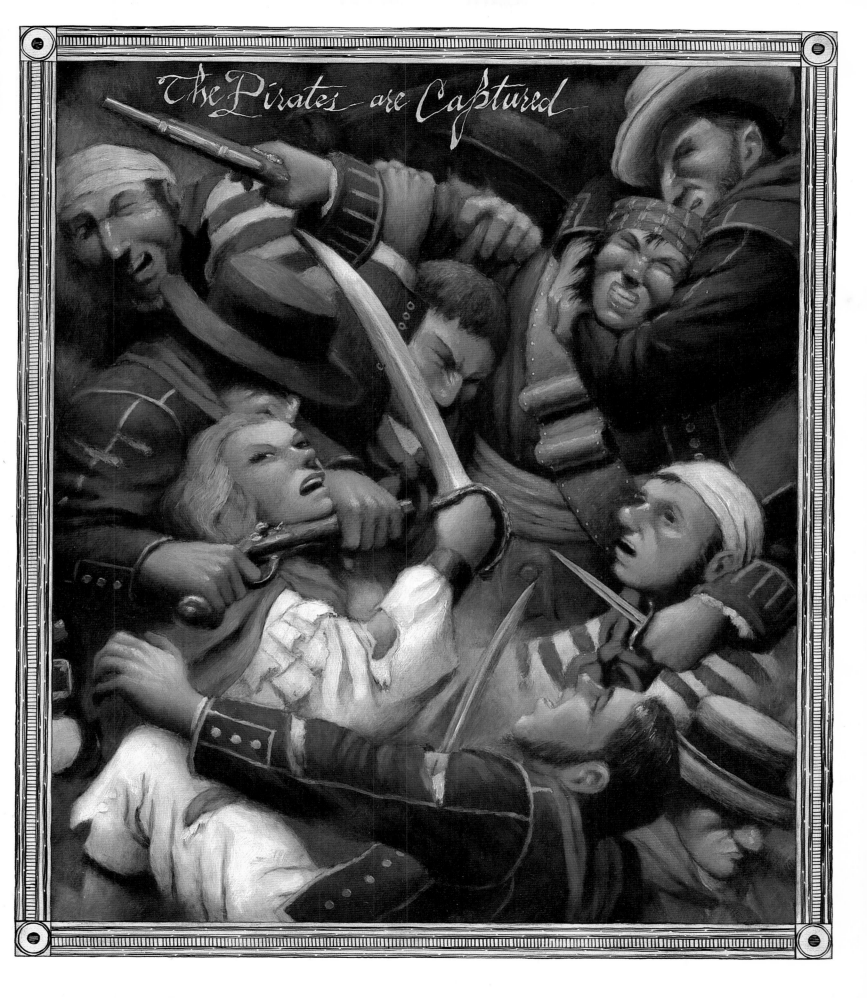

The Pirates are Captured

And silver the coins and silver the moon,
Silver the waves on the top of the sea,
When the pirate ship comes sailing in,
That gallant *Vanity*.

The Vanity Burns

The winter seas were dark and cold
Around Jamaica isle
When Anne Bonney and Mary Reade
Were readied for their trial.

They marched along the prison walk;
They passed Jack's cell block by.
Called Anne: "If you'd fought like a man,
My Jack, you'd need not die.

"If you had fought right by my side,
This day we'd both be free,
A-sailing in the open air
All on the silver sea."

The pirate queens before the judge
Each pleaded for her life.
"I am about to have a child;
I am a pirate's wife."

"Oh, you may be a pirate's wife,
Or by a man beguiled,
But never would I hang a maid
And kill the sinless child."

So Calico Jack and all his crew
Hanged on the gallows tree,
But bonny Anne and Mary Reade
Were by the judge set free.

Pleading their Bellies

Gallows Point ~

And silver the coins and silver the moon,
Silver the waves on the top of the sea,
When the pirate ship comes sailing in,
That gallant *Vanity*.

Port Royal, Jamaica

And they say still on autumn nights
In Port Maria Bay,
Where tunny fish all leap and sport
Around the bustling cay,

A ghostly ship sails to and fro
Above the silver waves.
Then Jack and all his coward crew
Rise anxious from their graves

To sail the endless ocean round.
No! Never a rest get they.
But Anne and Mary's children's children
Round their households play.

Granny Annie   Grandma Mary

The Ghost Ship Vanity

And silver the coins and silver the moon,
Silver the waves on the top of the sea,
When the ghostly ship comes sailing in,
That gallant *Vanity*.

Author's Note

Anne Bonney (or Bonny) and **Mary Reade** were women pirates who sailed with "Calico Jack" Rackham's crew in the sloop *Vanity* along the coasts of America in the 1700s. In fact, they were the most famous women pirates in the world. Stories about their trial on November 20, 1720, filled the penny papers and news sheets of the day.

Captain Jonathan Barnet's man-of-war *Albion* captured the *Vanity* because only Anne and Mary were up on deck and willing to fight. The men were below, drinking rum and playing cards with nine turtle fishermen they had captured that day.

Anne visited her husband, Rackham, in prison and said to him: "I am sorry to see you there, but if you had fought like a man, you need not be hanged like a dog." Then she walked away.

She and Mary Reade "pleaded their bellies," meaning they were pregnant. Some say Mary died in prison and that Anne's father got her off free. She settled down as a poor but honest housewife with two children on a small Caribbean island. Others say Mary did not die but feigned death and was carried out of prison in a shroud. Still others, that both Anne and Mary were set free by the judge, then moved to Louisiana, where they raised their children and were friends to the end of their lives.

We can only imagine the stories they must have told at bedtime.